Another 17 Prehistoric Monsters

EVERYONE SHOULD KNOW ABOUT

STANTON F. FINK

VOLUME XIII OF STANTON'S COLORING BOOKS

Acknowledgments

and Dedication

To my father, in whose books I discovered my first monsters.

To Will Caligan, whose help and encouragement is one of the primary reasons for this coloring book's existence.

To Mariano Silvera, who should have had his own artbooks

To Doctor David Morafka, who helped teach me to be more picky with my information.

To my friends, who helped push me to make this.

Table of Contents

Introduction

The purpose of this coloring book series is to provide information on various prehistoric animals both profoundly famous and incredibly obscure to artists of all ages. Of course, there is a lot of material to work with, as animals have been a major component of Earth's ecosystems for at least 670 million years.

For the sake of space and workability, each volume will contain 17 entries: ideally, one species for each geological time period, if possible. If you, or your inner and or outer child do not see your favorite prehistoric animal here, it may be eventually featured in another volume. Or, contact me to have it put into a later volume.

Glossary

- **Aquatic**- Living in water.
- **Arthropod**- Any member of the animal phylum Arthropoda, including trilobites, arachnids, crustaceans, insects, myriapods and their relatives. All arthropods have armor-like, jointed exoskeletons made of chitin-derived plates, sometimes reinforced with calcium carbonate, and jointed limbs.
- **Cambrian**- A period of time in the Paleozoic Era from 541 to 485 million years ago.
- **Carboniferous**- A period of time in the Paleozoic Era from 359 to 300 million years ago.
- **Cenozoic**- An era of time in the Phanerozoic Eon from 65 million years ago until now.
- **Chordate**- Any member of the animal phylum Chordata, including sea squirts, lancet fish, and vertebrates (such as lampreys, sharks, tuna, frogs, lizards, chickens, and people). All chordates have, at least at some point in their life cycle, a notochord, a long, flexible rod, usually made of cartilage, or, in the case of most vertebrates, cartilage and bone, running down the back from head to tail, directly beneath the neural tube.
- **Cnidarian**- Any member of the animal phylum Cnidaria, such as jellyfish, box jellies, Portuguese Man'o'war, sea anemones, coral and the parasitic myxozoans. Cnidarians are usually radially symmetrical, and have unique, venom-injecting stinging cells called "cnidocytes."
- **Cretaceous**- The last period of time in the Mesozoic Era, from 144 to 66 million years ago.
- **Devonian-** A period of time in the Paleozoic Era from 414 to 360 million years ago.
- **Ediacaran**- The last period of time in the Precambrian Eon from 635 to 542 million years ago.
- **Eocene**- A period of time in the Cenozoic Era from 55 to 33 million years ago.
- **Fauna**- In an ecological context, "fauna" refers to the animal components of an ecosystem.
- **Formation**- In a geological or paleontological context, a formation is a group of rock layers.
- **Gnathostome**- A gnathostome is any vertebrate chordate with a moveable jaw (or had an ancestor with one).
- **Holocene**- A period of time in the Cenozoic Era from 12,000 years ago until now.
- **_Incertae sedis_-** A Latin phrase literally meaning "uncertain seat." "_Incertae sedis_" is a term in classification used to refer to a species or group whose relationships with related organisms are unclear or poorly defined.
- **Jurassic**- The second period of time in the Mesozoic Era, from 199 to 145 million years ago.
- **Mesozoic**- An era of time in the Phanerozoic Eon from 249 to 66 million years ago.
- **Miocene**- A period of time in the Cenozoic Era from 23 to 5 million years ago.

- **Mollusk**- Any member of the animal phylum Mollusca, including snails, clams, squid, octopuses, tusk shells and chitons. Most mollusks have a calcium carbonate shell, and a toothed, file-like tongue called a radula. All mollusks have a cape-like organ, the mantle, which usually secretes the shell, and houses breathing organs, and a nervous system.
- **Nekton**- Any aquatic animal that lives either entirely or almost entirely in the water column, and relies on its own swimming or propulsion abilities to keep and move itself in and around the water column. Anchovies, porpoises and ichthyosaurs are examples of nekton.
- **Neogene**- The second third of the Cenozoic Era, comprising of the Miocene and the Pliocene periods.
- **Oligocene**- A period of time in the Cenozoic Era from 33 to 23 million years ago.
- **Ordovician**- A period of time in the Paleozoic Era from 484 to 440 million years ago.
- **Paleocene**- A period of time in the Cenozoic Era from 65 to 55 million years ago.
- **Paleogene**- The first third of the Cenozoic Era, comprising of the Paleocene, Eocene, and Oligocene.
- **Paleozoic**- An era of time in the Phanerozoic Eon from 249 to 66 million years ago.
- **Permian**- The last period of time in the Paleozoic Era, the time of "The Great Dying," or most severe of all known extinction events, from 299 to 250 million years ago.
- **Pharynx**- A structure in the throat of many animals located directly behind the mouth or oral chamber. In vertebrates, it often houses breathing structures, like gills.
- **Plankton**- An organism that uses water currents and waterflow to as its primary means of transportation in the water column because it is either too small to move long distances by its own power, or lacks the ability to propel itself entirely. Sargassum seaweed and jellyfish are two varieties of plankton.
- **Pleistocene**- A period of time in the Cenozoic Era from 3 million years ago until 12 thousand years ago.
- **Pliocene**- A period of time in the Cenozoic Era from 5 to 3 million years ago.
- **Quaternary**- The last third of the Cenozoic Era, comprising of the Pleistocene and the Holocene periods.
- **Terrestrial**- Living on land.
- **Triassic**- The first period of time in the Mesozoic Era, from 249 to 200 million years ago.

Name	Trilobite Proarticulatan
Species	*Archaeaspinus fedonkini*
Phylum	Proarticulata
Class	Cephalozoa
Size	4 to 9 millimeters
Time Period	Late Ediacaran of the Precambrian, 555 million years ago
Location	Zimnii Bereg and Kharakhta of the White Sea, Russia, and Chace Range of the Flinders Ranges, Australia.

Comments

The Trilobite Proarticulatan, *Archaeaspinus fedonkini*, is a tiny, arthropod-like creature closely related to the Yorga Proarticulatan, *Yorgia waggoneri*, and the Sigil Proarticulatan, *Praecambridium sigillum.* The trilobite proarticulatan, originally described as *"Archaeaspis" fedonkini*, was first discovered along the Winter Coast of the White Sea, in Russia, where, during the Precambrian, it lived in a diverse, marine community with other proarticulatans.

Around the same time the Russian specimens were found, Australian scientists discovered fossils of what they thought were tiny, trilobite-like arthropods amongst the Flinders Ediacaran organisms. However, as soon as Russian researchers examined the "Flinders soft-bodied trilobites," they immediately recognized them as *Archaeaspinus*.

As a bit of further irony, the name *"Archaeaspis"* could not be used as the scientific name for the trilobite proarticulatan as that name was already in use for a genus of very primitive redlichiid trilobite found in Lower Cambrian Siberian and Californian marine strata.

Name

Atlantic Ancient Cupsponge

Species   *Archaeocyathus atlanticus*

Phylum   Porifera

Subphylum   Archaeocyatha

Class   Irregulares

Order   Archaeocyathida

Family   Archaeocyathidae

Size   Each cup about about 2 centimeters in diamters

Time Period   "Stage 4" to "Stage 5" of the Cambrian, 517 to 510 million years ago

Location   Labrador, Canada

Comments   The Atlantic Ancient Cupsponge, *Archaeocyathus atlanticus*, is the first described species of a diverse group of extinct, sponge-like organisms that built the first known animal-derived reefs in tropical and subtropical, shallow-water marine environments throughout the world during the Early to Middle Cambrian. Archaeocyathans ("ancient cups") differ from the related sponges in that the archaeocyathan skeleton was, instead of a network of protein fibers and either calcium carbonate or silica spicules, a series of conical, porous, calcium carbonate walls.

As mentioned earlier, many species of archaeocyathans, the Atlantic ancient cupsponge included, built reefs, termed "bio-herms." Individuals grew together, and then on top of the corpses of earlier individuals in such abundant stacks that they would eventually form huge mounds built out of the skeletons of individuals and trapped sediment. The Atlantic ancient cupsponge formed bio-herms in what is now Labrador, Canada (thus it being named after an ocean that would not exist until four-hundred million years after its extinction).

Name

Crested Sea Canteen

Species	*Platycystites cristatus*
Phylum	Echinodermata
Class	Paracrinoidea
Order	Platycystitida
Family	Platycystitidae
Size	Body over 4.5 centimeters tall.
Time Period	Blackriverian Stage of the Middle Ordovician, probably about 462 to 459 million years ago
Location	Mountain Lake Member of the Bromide Formation, Arbuckle Mountains, and Criner Hills of Oklahoma

Comments

The Crested Sea Canteen, *Platycystites cristatus*, is an extinct paracrinoid, a superficially sea lily-like echinoderm that lived in shallow-water marine environments in what is now the state of Oklahoma. Paracrinoids were stalked echinoderms that either assymetrical, or somewhat bilaterally symmetrical, and were notable, if not important members of marine communities of Ordovician United States, though there were a few that lived in Sweden.

While the crested sea canteen had a stalk, its own body, or theca, is so comparatively massive (as massive as an animal the size and shape of an apricot pit can be), and its stalk so feeble, that researchers believe that the adult lived with its stalk buried in the substrate.

Name   Serpenthorn Nautiloid

Species	*Ophioceras simplex*
Phylum	Mollusca
Class	Cephalopoda
Subclass	Nautiloidea
Order	Tarphycerida
Family	Ophidioceratidae
Size	Shell up to 2 centimeters in diameter
Time Period	Ludlow epoch of the Late Silurian, 427 to 423 million years ago
Location	Great Britain and Norway
Comments	The Serpenthorn Nautiloid, *Ophioceras simplex*, is an extinct, ammonite-like nautiloid cephalopod from the Late Silurian of Bohemia. Its shell coils into a disc where, in the adult shell, the youngest whorl unwinds from the main body, and sticks out. The shell opening, in the adult form, is constricted to form a T-shape. The serpenthorn nautiloid probably hunted smaller animals and possibly foraminifera.

Name Laurel Nautiloid

Species	*Lorieroceras lorieri*
Phylum	Mollusca
Class	Cephalopoda
Subclass	Nautiloidea
Order	Oncocerida
Family	Nothoceratidae
Size	Complete shell probably about 8 centimeters tall.
Time Period	Lochkovian to Pragian epochs of the Early Devonian, from 491 to 407 million years ago.
Location	Courtoisieres, Department of Sarthe, France

Comments

The Laurel Nautiloid, *Lorieroceras lorieri*, is a bizarre nautiloid from the Lower Devonian of Courtoisieres, France. The laurel nautiloid's shell is a loosely-coiled, turban-shaped helix, a form rarely seen in nautiloids in general. The shell opening is constricted into a T-shape. Needless to say, the laurel nautiloid was probably a very poor swimmer.

Here, the laurel nautiloid is shown with a pair of *Protopteraspis* pteraspidid heterostracans.

Name

(Arkansas) Flying Nautilid

Species	*Solenochilus springeri*
Phylum	Mollusca
Class	Cephalopoda
Subclass	Nautiloidea
Order	Nautilida
Family	Solenochilidae
Size	"Wingspan" about 26 centimeters wide
Time Period	Early Pennsylvanian epoch of the Carboniferous, about 315 million years ago
Location	Arkansas, United States

Comments

The Flying Nautilids of genus *Solenochilus* are an extinct group of nautilids related to the modern nautiluses of Nautilidae.

In mature individualss of Solenochilidae, the rim of the shell opening near the umbilicus (where the shell whorls coil around) extend out into exaggerated, wing-like spines. The functions of these spines remain unknown, though they may have had roles in altering their owner's hydrodynamics, species-recognition, or even to discourage predators.

Solenochilus springeri is found in Early Pennsylvanian-aged marine strata of Carboniferous Arkansas.

Name

Sixhorned Misnomer

Species	*Tetraceratops insignis*
Phylum	Chordata
clade	Sphenacodontoidea
Order	Therapsida
Family	*incertae sedis*
Size	Holotype skull about 9 centimeters long
Time Period	Leonardian or Kungurian Stage of the Cisuralian Epoch of the Early to early Middle Permian, 274 million years ago.
Location	Clear Fork group of the Big Witchita River formation, Baylor County, Texas

Comments

The Sixhorned Misnomer, *Tetraceratops insignis*, is the earliest known therapsid, the oldest known member of a group of tetrapod vertebrates ancestral to mammals: effectively, the sixhorned misnomer is the first "paramammal." By coincidence, the sixhorned misnomer is also the earliest known tetrapod with horns.

When the holotype skull, and so far, only known specimen was discovered, much of the matrix it was embedded in was not yet removed due to it being a very hard rock, leaving only two pairs of horns, one pair on the prefrontal bones and one pair on the premaxillae bones, exposed. Later researchers were able to successfully remove more of the matrix, exposing a third pair of horns on the corners of its mandible. In life, the living animal would have looked vaguely like a monitor lizard with four horns on its snout, and a pair of spines emanating from the corners of its jaw.

The long, fang-like teeth clearly mark the sixhorned misnomer as a predator; one that undoubtedly preyed on smaller animals, such as amphibians and primitive reptiles.

Name   Wickertrapper

Species	*Gerrothorax pulcherimus*
Phylum	Chordata
Class	Amphibia
Order	Temnospondyli
Family	Plagiosauridae
Size	Body about 1 meter long
Time Period	Ladnian to Rhaetian epochs of the Triassic Period, 238 to 203 million years ago
Location	Germany, Sweden, Greenland, Thailand

Comments

The Wickertrapper, *Gerrothorax pulcherimus*, is a wide-ranging species of aquatic temnospondyl amphibian that lived at the bottoms of freshwater systems in Pangaea corresponded to Europe, Greenland and possibly Thailand during much of the Triassic Period.

The wickertrapper was superbly adapted for life as a benthic predator, as it spent most of its time as an adult with its flattened body half-buried in sediment while visually scanning for prey with its large eyes. Unlike most gnathostomes, who open their mouths by lowering the mandible, the wickertrapper opened its mouth by lifting its head, similar to how humans lift up a toilet lid. The wickertrapper most likely threw its head up with enough swiftness to generate a suction force to pull suitable prey into its mouth to be bitten and or swallowed.

Name

Disaster Valentine Urchin

Species	*Cardiolampas friburgensis*
Phylum	Echinodermata
Class	Echinoidea
Superorder	Atelostomata
(basal) Family	Collyritidae
Size	Test about 5 centimeters long
Time Period	Late Oxfordian epoch of the Late Jurassic, about 159 to 157 million years ago.
Location	Europe and Tunisia.

Comments

The Disaster Valentine Urchin, *Cardiolampas friburgensis*, is an extinct burrowing sea urchin related to the modern-day heart urchins. Its fossils are found in late Jurassic marine strata in Tunisia and various localities in Europe, especially, but not restricted to France.

Although it belongs to the same group, Atelostomata, as the heart urchins, the disaster Valentine is more closely related to other Jurassic and Cretaceous-aged atelostomates, like those of the genera *Disaster* and *Collyrites*.

The test or shell of the disaster Valentine was a mound sculpted into a heart, similar to the shape of a Valentine's Day chocolate heart. The tiny mouth was located beneath the divet between the two lobes of the "heart."

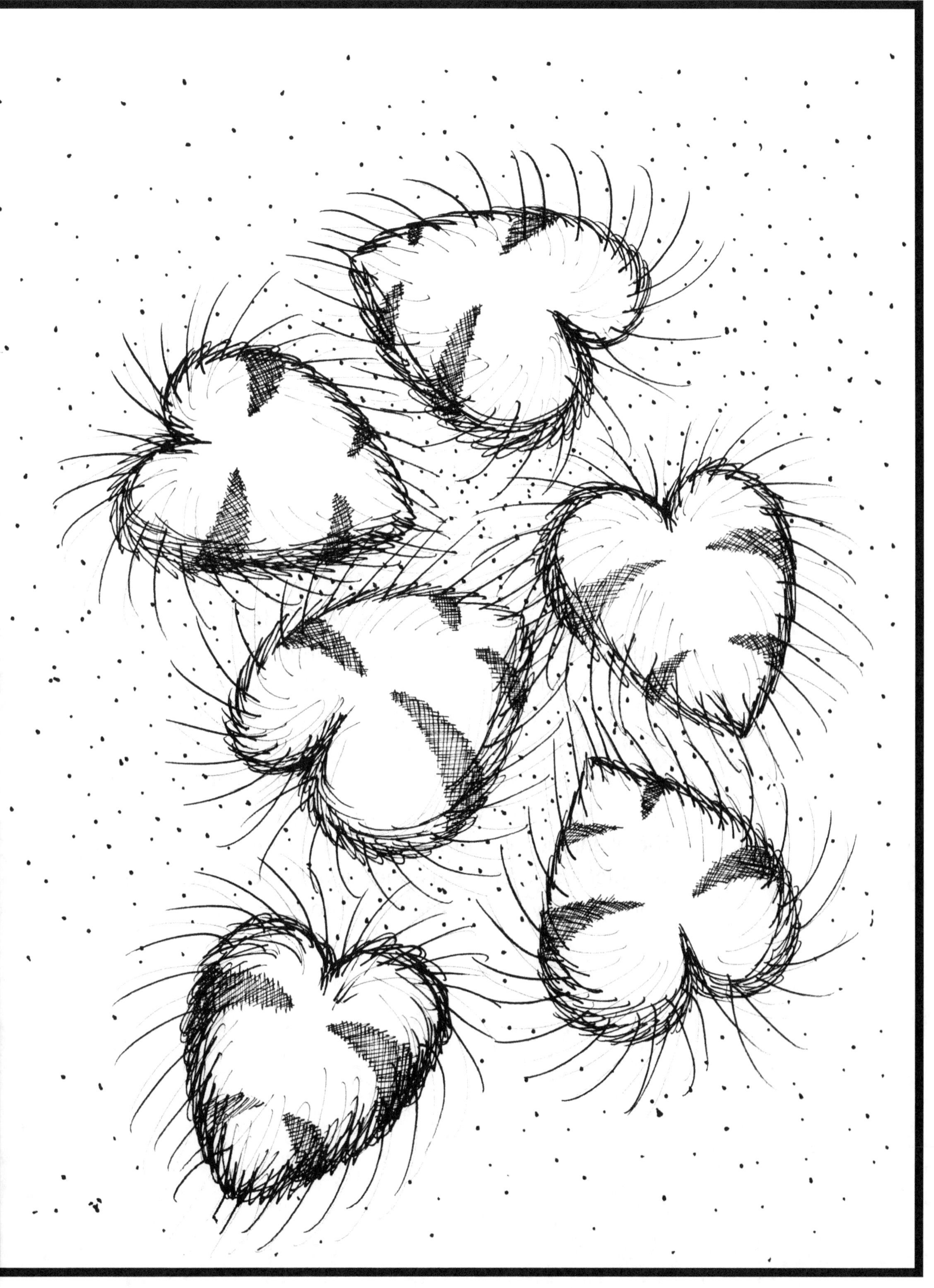

Name	Alienroach
Species	*Alienopterus brachyelytrus*
Phylum	Arthropoda
Class	Insecta
Order	Alienoptera
Family	Alienopteridae
Size	Holotype and only-known specimen about 14 millimeters long
Time Period	Cenomanian Epoch of the Middle Cretaceous Period, 99 million years ago.
Location	Hukawng Valley, Myanmar

Comments

The Alienroach, *Alienopterus brachyelytrus*, is a peculiar, tiny, predatory insect descended from cockroaches. It is apparently a "dead end" in the spectrum between cockroaches and mantids, as it has features shared with cockroaches, Cretaceous-aged mantid-like cockroaches and mantids, but, also has its own unique features that demonstrate it has no living descendants of its own.

Chief among its unique features are its wings: the first pair, or forewings, are modified into shoulderpad-like structures similar to the forewings-turned-elytra of beetles.

The alienroach is currently known only from a male trapped in a piece of Cretaceous-aged amber from Myanmar, where it originally lived in a tropical rainforest.

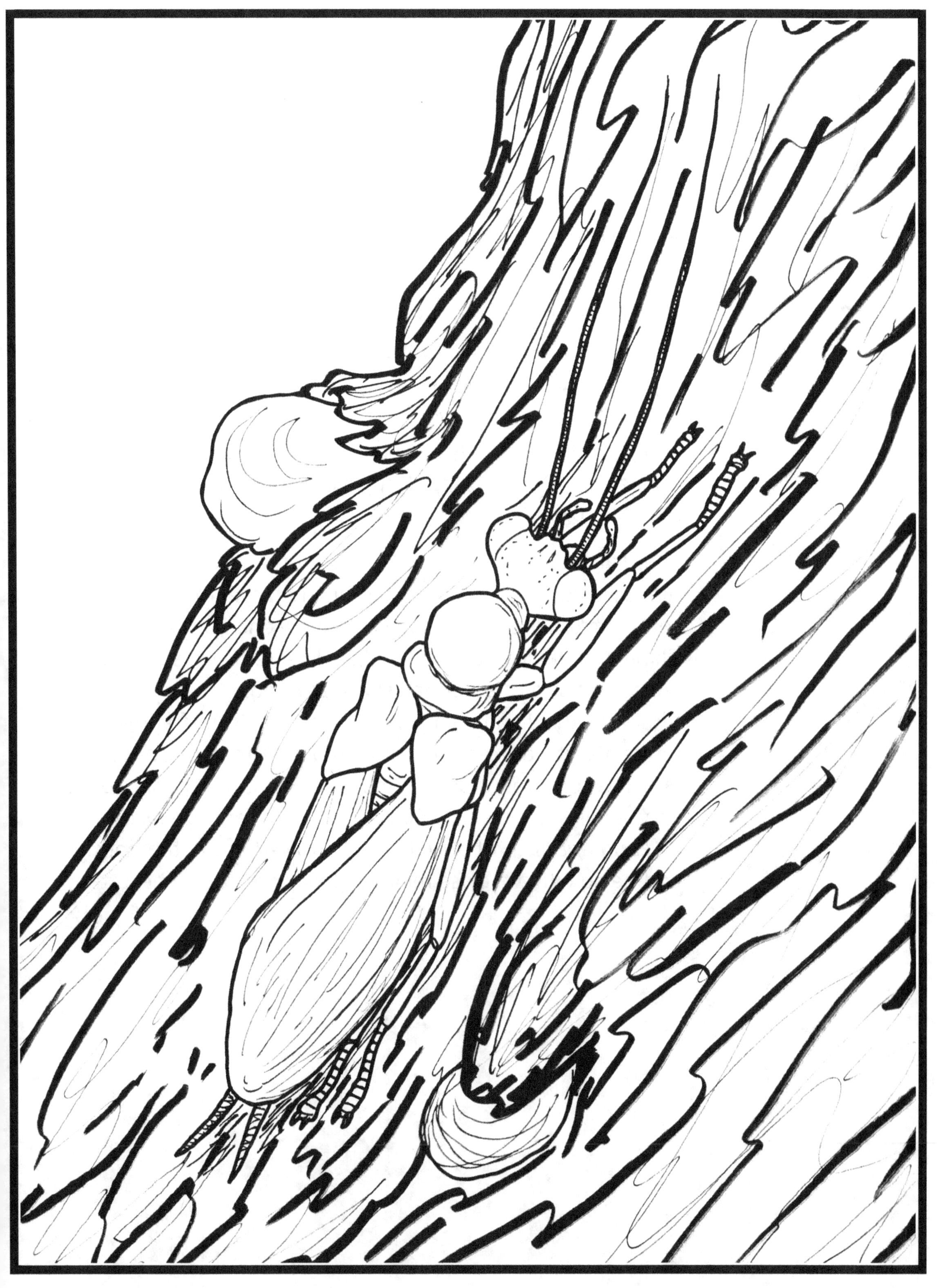

Name	Jiangxi Lang
Species	*Jiangxia chaotoensis*
Phylum	Chordata
Class	Mammalia
Order	Mesonychia
Family	Mesonychidae
Size	Probably similar in size to a German shepherd
Time Period	Nongshanian or Thanetian Epoch of the Late Paleocene, about 59 to 56 million years ago
Location	Wanshi Member of the Upper Chijiang Formation near the village of Qiaotoucun, Qinglong Commune, Dayu Co., Jiangxi Province, China
Comments	

The Jiangxi Lang, 江 西 狼 , *Jiangxia chaotoensis*, is a mesonychid known from a fragment of a mandible, and some broken teeth found in Late Paleocene Jiangxi Province, China (for which it is named). The remains suggest an animal the size of a German shephard dog.

Although the Jiangxi lang is known only from fragmentary remnants, it still can be compared to other mesonychids, and relationships drawn. The Jiangxi lang appears to be very similar to mesonychids of the genera *Dissacus* and *Hukoutherium*, probably having evolved from the former, and being either a close relative of, or ancestor to the latter.

Name   Wyoming Anole

Species	*Afairiguana avius*
Phylum	Chordata
Class	Reptilia
Order	Squamata
Suborder	Iguania
Family	Iguanidae
Subfamily	Polychrotinae
Size	Holotype skeleton about 7 to 8 centimeters long.
Time Period	Ypresian Epoch of the Eocene Period, 52 to 51 million years ago
Location	Fossil Lake, Warfield Locality of the Fossil Butte Member, Green River Formation, Wyoming
Comments	The Wyoming Anole, *Afairiguana avius*, shown here compared to the extinct monitor lizard, *Saniwa,* is the earliest known iguanian lizard from the Western Hemisphere that can be placed within a specific subgroup of Iguanidae. In this case, the subfamily of anoles, Polychrotinae.

The Wyoming anole is the northernmost known anole, well away from the primary centers of anole diversity in the Caribbean and South America. Compared to modern-day anoles, the Wyoming anole was sort of puny-headed. Other details of the skeletal anatomy show that it could autotomize, or shed its tail if necessary, like most iguanids can.

Name

(Karl Alfred von Zittel's) Arsinoeceros

Species	*Arsinoitherium zitteli*
Phylum	Chordata
Class	Mammalia
Order	Embrithopoda
Family	Arsinotheriidae
Size	About 1.75 meters at the shoulder
Time Period	Late Eocene to Early Oligocene, from 36 to 30 million years ago
Location	Mangrove forests in what is now the Fayum Oasis, Egypt

Comments

The (Karl Alfred von Zittel's) Arsinoeceros, *Arsinoitherium zitteli*, is a superficially rhinoceros-like mammal related to living afrotheres like elephants, sirenians and tenrecs. The various species of arsinoeceros, named after the Ptolemaic Queen Arsinoe I, lived in Northeastern Africa during the Eocene and early Oligocene. Zittel's arsinoeceros, named after the eminent German palaeontogist and father of Egyptian palaeontogy, is the best known and studied, as complete skeletons have been recovered from the Fayum Oasis which was, back during the middle Paleogene, a massive mangrove swamp bordering the Tethys Ocean.

The most distinctive feature of the arsinoeceros is the first pair of large, blade-like horns, these horns may have been used for intimidation and intraspecies signalling. The skulls show that they had the primitive mammallian full compliment of 44 teeth: this suggests the living animals were herbivorous browsers that selectively fed on soft vegetation.

The pair of fanged animals in the trees are a pair of mysterious, extinct afrotheres, *Ptolemaia grangeri*, that were, in the course of their study by humans, successively (mis)identified as a monkey, and a wolf-sized shrew (among the better known failed attempts at identifying them).

Name

Plā duk wāḷ

Species *Cetopangasius chaetobranchus*

Phylum Chordata

Class Actinopterygii

Order Siluriformes

Family Pangasiidae

Size Holotype 34.5 centimeters long, living animal may be 35 centimeters long in average.

Time Period Middle to Late Miocene, 14 to 5 million years ago

Location Phetchabun Lake, Ban Nong Pla, Phetchabun Province of Thailand

Comments The Pla duk wal ("whale catfish"), *Cetopangasius chaetobranchus*, is an extinct pangasiid catfish that lived in an extinct lake in what is now Phetchabun Province in Thailand.

The pla duk wal differs from other pangasiids in that its head is disproportionally larger in comparison to other pangasiids, and that it had almost all of its gill-rakers modified for filter-feeding. Most other pangasiids are either herbivorous or molluscivores.

Phetchabun Lake was originally in a flood plain that drained into a valley system that is now the Gulf of Siam. The lake was surrounded by forests of magnolia trees, and supported turtles and a diverse fish fauna of carps and catfishes, the pla duk wal included. The borders of the lake are thought to have expanded during the rainy season and contracted during the dry season.

Name

South American Leopard Seal

Species — *Acrophoca longirostris*

Phylum — Chordata

Class — Mammalia

Order — Carnivoria

Family — Phocidae

Size — About 1.5 meters long

Time Period — Late Miocene to Early Pliocene

Location — Pacific coasts of Peru to Chile

Comments — The South American Leopard Seal, *Acrophoca longirostris*, is an ancestor of the modern Leopard Seal, *Hydrurga leptonyx,* which lives in Antarctica. The South American leopard seal lived along the Pacific coast of South America, in what are now the countries of Peru and Chile.

The skeleton shows an animal not as streamlined as the modern leopard seal, with fins that are not as finely adapted to manevourable swimming as its descendant. This suggests that *Acrophoca* spent more time on land than *Hydrurga* does, and probably did not hunt swift prey like penguins and seals like the modern leopard seal.

Acrophoca most likely exclusively preyed on fish, as, in addition to it not being adapted to hunt other seals or sea birds effectively, its teeth lack the fringes seen in leopard seals that allow them to eat krill.

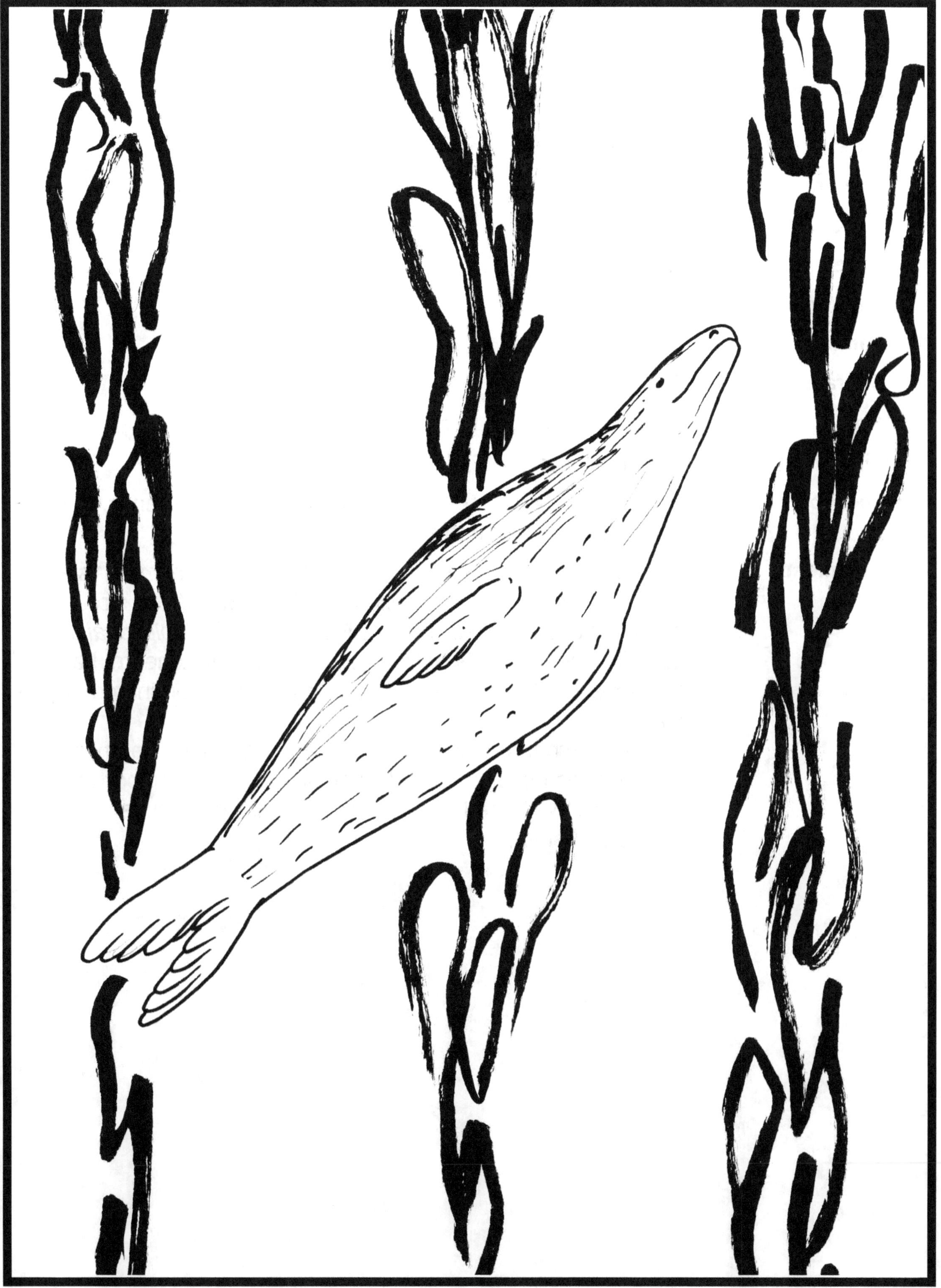

Name

Blunt-snouted Dolphin

Species	*Platalearostrum hoekmani*
Phylum	Chordata
Class	Mammalia
Order	Artiodactyla
Infraorder	Cetacea
Family	Delphinidae
Subfamily	Orcininae
Size	Comparable in size to a large pilot whale
Time Period	Middle Pliocene to Early Pleistocene
Location	The North Sea, off the coast of the Netherlands, 110 kilometers west of Rotterdam.
Comments	The Blunt-snouted Dolphin, *Platalearostrum hoekmani*, is an extinct, medium to large-sized delphinid whale, or oceanic dolphin closely related to the pilot whales of *Globicephala*. It lived in the North Sea from the Middle Pliocene to Early Pleistocene, back when that area was dominated by walruses. The blunt-snouted dolphin is known from jaw fragments, and a spoon-shaped snout that would have supported a huge, pillow-shaped melon (the organ of echolation in toothed whales).

Name

(Georg Wilhelm) Steller's Sea Cow

Species	*Hydrodamalis gigas*
Phylum	Chordata
Class	Mammalia
Order	Sirenia
Family	Dugongidae
Size	Up to 9 meters
Time Period	Pleistocene to Holocene: last confirmed sightings in 1768 AD
Location	Last known population lived in the Commander Islands, may have ranged from Honshu, Japan to Monterey Bay, California during the Pleistocene.

Comments

The Steller's Sea Cow, *Hydrodamalis gigas*, is an extinct dugong, and is the largest known sirenian. During the Pleistocene, the Steller's sea cow ranged throughout the Northern Pacific, with bones found in Honshu, various islands in the Bering Sea, easternmost Siberia, Alaska and Monterey Bay, California. The Steller's sea cow was discovered by Europeans in 1741 when the crew of the *St Peter*, of Vitus Bering's Second Kamchatka Expedition, was shipwrecked on what is now known as Bering Island. Steller is the only human observer to have made detailed notes about the living animal's anatomy and behavior.

Unlike other sirenians, the Steller's sea cow had no teeth, using, instead, long, stiff bristles on its upper lip in conjunction with keratinous pads in its mouth to tear off and chew pieces of kelp. It had very thick blubber to insulate it from the frigid cold water: tragically, humans found sea cow blubber to be delicious. The thick skin was rough, and often pitted with craters formed by parasites. The underside of its flippers also had bristles. The Steller's sea cow was a social animal, and swam together in herd-like groups. According to Steller's notes, when Russian sailors attacked an individual with harpoons, its herdmates would then attempt to rescue their comrade by trying to nudge the harpoon out, while circling to keep their wounded friend from drowning.

After Bering's expedition, Russian sailors used the Bering Strait to travel to Alaska and North America, and would hunt the Steller's sea cow for meat and blubber. Twenty-seven years after its discovery by Europeans, the Steller's sea cow was no longer seen, presumed extinct.

Bibliography

- Amson, Eli, and Michel Laurin. "On the affinities of *Tetraceratops insignis*, an Early Permian synapsid." *Acta Palaeontologica Polonica* 56.2 (2011): 301-312.
- Bai, Ming, et al. "† Alienoptera—A new insect order in the roach–mantodean twilight zone." *Gondwana Research* 39 (2016): 317-326.
- Conrad, Jack L., Olivier Rieppel, and Lance Grande. "A Green River (Eocene) polychrotid (Squamata: Reptilia) and a re-examination of iguanian systematics." *Journal of Paleontology* 81.6 (2007): 1365-1373.
- Day, David. *The doomsday book of animals: a natural history of vanished species.* Penguin Putnam, 1981.
- Flannery, Tim Fridtjof, and Peter Schouten. *A gap in nature: discovering the world's extinct animals.* Atlantic Monthly Press, 2001.
- Hill, Dorothy. *Treatise on Invertebrate Paleontology: Archaeocyatha.* Geological Society of America, 1972.
- Ivantsov, A. Yu. "*Vendia* and Other Precambrian 'Arthropods'," Paleontol. Zh., No. 4, 3–10 (2001) [Paleontol. J. 35 (3), 233–240 (1999)].
- Ivantsov, A. Yu. "New Proarticulata from the Vendian of the Arkhangelsk Region," Paleontol. Zh., No. 3, 21–26 (2004b) [Paleontol. J. 38 (3), 247–253 (2004b)].
- Jenkins Jr, Farish A., et al. "Gerrothorax pulcherrimus from the Upper Triassic Fleming Fjord Formation of East Greenland and a reassessment of head lifting in temnospondyl feeding." *Journal of Vertebrate Paleontology* 28.4 (2008): 935-950.
- Laurin, Michel, and Robert R. Reisz. "*Tetraceratops* is the oldest known therapsid." *Nature* 345.6272 (1990): 249-250.
- Laurin, Michel, and Robert R. Reisz. "The osteology and relationships of *Tetraceratops insignis,* the oldest known therapsid." *Journal of Vertebrate Paleontology* 16.1 (1996): 95-102.
- Moore, R. C. "Treatise on Invertebrate Paleontology. Part K, Mollusca 3, Cephalopoda." *Geological Society of America and University of Kansas, New York and Lawrence, Kansas* (1964).
- Moore, Raymond Cecil, ed. *Treatise on Invertebrate Paleontology: Part U: Echinodermata 3, Asterozoa-Echinozoa.* Geological society of America, 1966.
- Muizon, C. de. 1981. Les vertébrés fossiles de la Formation Pisco (Pérou). Première partie: deux nouveaux Monachinae (Phocidae, Mammalia) du Pliocène de Sud-Sacaco. Travaux de l'Institut Français d'Études Andines 22:1-1
- Parsley, Ronald L., and Leigh W. Mintz. *North American Paracrinoidea:(Ordovician, Paracrinozoa, new, Echinodermata).* Paleontological Research Institution, 1975.
- Post, Klaas, and Erwin JO Kompanje. "A new dolphin (Cetacea, Delphinidae) from the Plio-Pleistocene of the North Sea." *Deinsea* 14.1 (2010): 1-14.
- Prothero, Donald R. *After the dinosaurs: the age of mammals.* Indiana University Press, 2006.

- Roberts, Tyson R., and Junya Jumnongthai. "Miocene fishes from Lake Phetchabun in north-central Thailand, with descriptions of new taxa of Cyprinidae, Pangasiidae and Chandidae." *Natural History Bulletin of the Siam Society* 47 (1999): 153-189.
- Schoch, Rainer R., and Florian Witzmann. "Cranial morphology of the plagiosaurid Gerrothorax pulcherrimus as an extreme example of evolutionary stasis." *Lethaia* 45.3 (2012): 371-385.
- Turner, Alan, and Mauricio Antón. *Evolving Eden: an illustrated guide to the evolution of the African large-mammal fauna.* Columbia University Press, 2004.
- Zhang, Yuping, et al. "Several species of Condylarthra from the Paleocene of Jiangxi." (1997).

About the Artist

Stanton F. Fink is a student of Biology and Chinese Medicine, and makes a hobby of drawing monsters and researching flowers, arcane-looking creatures, prehistoric animals, fish, reptiles, birds and the occasional, really grotesque fungal fruiting body.

Stanton grew up and went to school in California and is currently living, drawing, and gardening in Oregon.

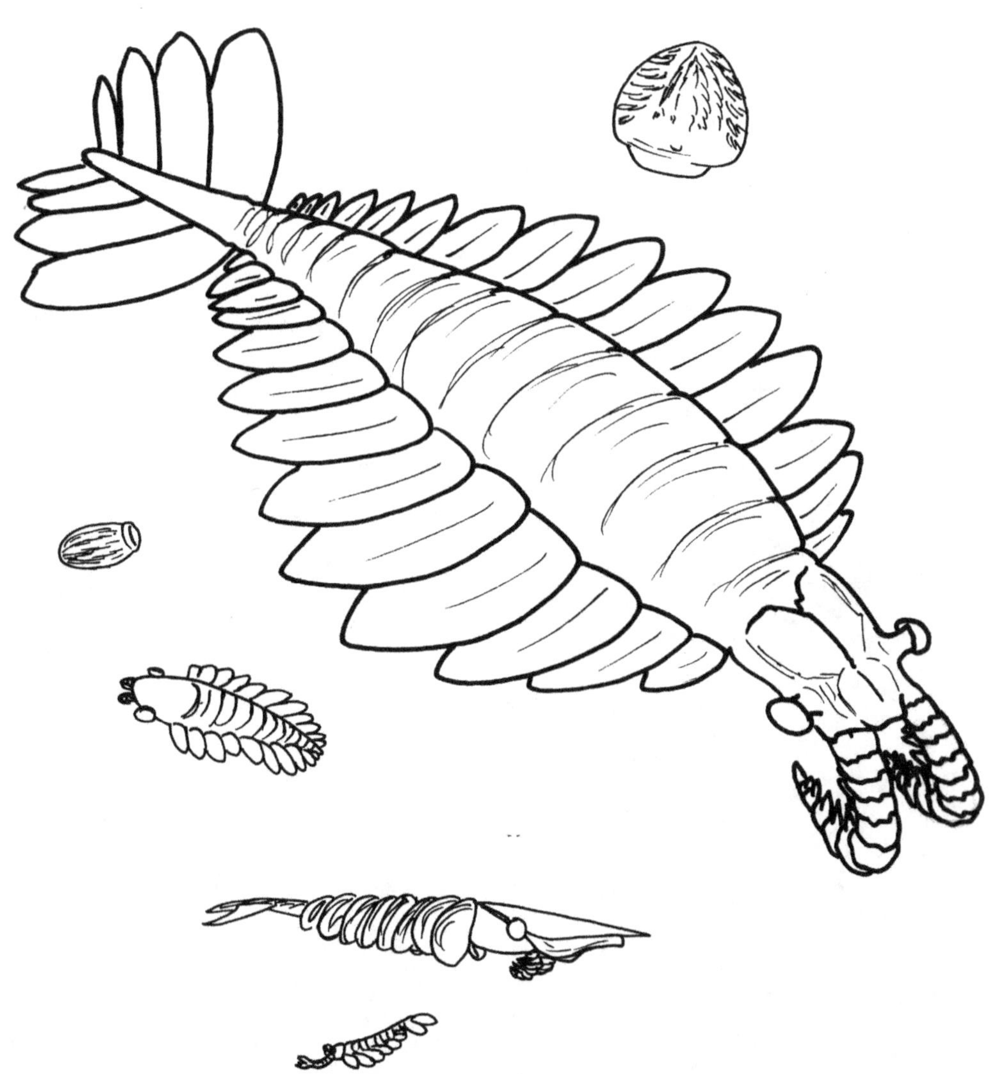